Clara C. Bolger

WESTFIELD

A Celebration of Community

WALTER CHOROSZEWSKI

WESTFIELD, *A Celebration of Community*

Designed by Walter Choroszewski
Printed in Korea
5 4 3 2 1

ISBN: 0-933605-14-5

AESTHETIC PRESS, INC.
P.O. Box 5306
Somerville, NJ 08876-1303

Web: www.aestheticpress.com
Email: info@aestheticpress.com
Telephone: 908 369-3777

WESTFIELD

A Celebration of Community

WALTER CHOROSZEWSKI

Produced in cooperation with
EDUCATION FUND OF WESTFIELD

AESTHETIC PRESS, INC.
Somerville, New Jersey

WESTFIELD *by* WALTER CHOROSZEWSKI

It all started as a dream (*literally!*) that I had just a few years ago. Through my career, I had photographed and produced many books and calendars about New Jersey as well as other regions; however, this dream seemed very clear to me —almost prophetic—that a book about Westfield was in my future.

A few months earlier I had photographed Westfield for New Jersey Monthly magazine, and through that assignment I developed a working relationship with Downtown Westfield Corporation (DWC). The morning after this dream I immediately called friends at DWC and asked them to schedule a meeting to discuss the possibility of using a Westfield book as a fund-raiser; unfortunately the proposal was never accepted by them.

I went on to produce a few other books before again speaking with friends at DWC who called me and asked if they could pass along my proposal to another town organization, the Education Fund of Westfield. After meeting with Darielle Walsh and her committees, I found a believer in the "dream." The book, WESTFIELD, *A Celebration of Community*, became a reality in 2003. The Education Fund of Westfield used the book project as a successful fund-raiser to provide additional resources that enhance the programs for students of the Westfield Public Schools.

Unlike my previous books, this book is unique in its focus on a smaller geographic area and is centered on the lives of the people within—essentially a photo-journalistic essay celebrating this vibrant community. The subtitle for this book was chosen because Westfield is the quintessential "community"—a word with origins meaning *fellowship* and *citizenry.* It is apparent that Westfield is a town of proud citizens who enjoy the fellowship of each other through participation in countless groups and organizations, many with a goal of serving the common good of Westfield.

The first pioneers of Westfield came from Long Island in the late 17th and early 18th centuries to settle the "west fields of Elizabethtown" but it was the organization of the Presbyterian Church in the late 1720s that truly established a sense of community. Westfield flourishes almost three hundred years later, and the Presbyterian Church continues to thrive as one of fifteen houses of worship active in the community today.

Westfield became a township in 1794; however, we are currently celebrating the centennial of Westfield becoming a "town" in 1903. No longer just rural farm fields located near the distant mountain fringe west of Elizabeth, larger than most villages but not quite a city, Westfield is clearly a "town"—complete with its own Town Clock, Town Bell Master, Town Crier and more!

Westfield has gained state and national recognition for its revitalized downtown. North and South Avenues along with Broad, Elm, Central, Prospect, and Quimby Streets, are all "Main" streets in the sense that they are filled with stores and restaurants that attract residents and visitors alike. Even traditional mall stores have set up shop and joined Westfield's active downtown community.

Encircling and radiating from the downtown is a residential community of tree-lined streets with handsome homes and beautiful gardens. With just over 10,000 households, many including young children, maintaining quality schools and an active sports program is a top priority.

Westfield is a town filled with a pride and passion for itself. Its residents *love* their community and it is this simple intangible that truly makes Westfield the special place it really is.

FRANCE
SERBIA
JAPAN
RUSSIA
GREAT
BRITAIN
BELGIUM
CHINA
RUMANIA
PORTUGAL
1917
WESTFIELD

The Plaza

Mindowaskin Lake

Train Station Lamps

Elm Street Cafe

Stoneleigh Park

Wychwood

Town Clock

Jack Panosh,
Town Bell Master &
Curator of Town Clock

Sam McCaulley, Town Crier

Mural,
Municipal Building

Chief Bernard Tracy
and members of
Westfield Police
Department

Municipal Building, Mindowaskin Lake

Downer Well Cap, Broad Street

Well House,
Woodland Avenue

Well House,
Miller-Cory
Museum

Wedding Photos, Mindowaskin Park

Arcanum Hall, Broad Street

Spring Gardens Tour,
Westfield Garden Club

The Education Fund of Westfield
hanks the Following Sponsors of the
Jill & Jack 5K Race
William B. Mercer, Inc.
PNC Bank
e Westfield Foundation
PASCO Investment Advisors, Inc.
ntury 21 Taylor & Love
artwells School Dining Services
arrocca Family
st Choice Personnel
The Side
iends of Westfield Track & Field
oles Family
aine Swingle, D.M.D.
onsall Chiropractice/Sports Centre
Ketcham Tax Services
Moto Photo
US Foodservice
Gerard Boyle Insurance
Galaxy Coach, Inc.
Clark Bagels
Great Harvest Bread Company

Jill & Jack Races,
Education Fund of Westfield

David Rowe, Conductor, and musicians from Westfield Symphony

Elias J. Zareva, Director,
and Westfield Community
Concert Band,
Mindowaskin Park

Westfield Tennis Club

Echo Lake

Beans

Bernie

Joe DiMaggio

Fuzzy

Rosie

Louie

Kelly

Zippy

Enu

Hopper

Temple Emanu-El

Redeemer Lutheran Church

St. Paul's Episcopal Church

First Baptist Church of Westfield

St. Helen's Roman Catholic Church

Roman Catholic Church of the Holy Trinity

Westfield
houses of worship

Rake and Hoe Garden Club,
Shadowlawn Garden

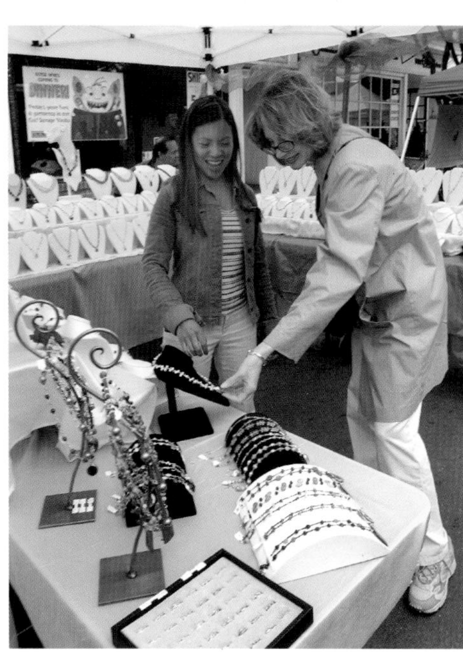

Downtown Street Fair,
Westfield Chamber of Commerce

Jazzfest,
Downtown Westfield
Corporation

Vicki's Diner

Ferraro's

Wind Mill

Haagen Dazs

Clyne & Murphy

Westfield eateries

Franklin Elementary

Tamaques Elementary

THOMAS ALVA EDISON INTERMEDIATE SCHOOL

Edison Intermediate

Washington Elementary

Jefferson Elementary

Wilson Elementary

Westfield
public schools

McKinley Elementary

Roosevelt Intermediate

Holy Trinity
Interparochial School

Westfield "Y" Child Care

Westfield Farmers Market

Miller-Cory Museum garden

Gladys Reimer, sculptor

Landscape Group,
Westfield Art Association,
Mindowaskin Park

DOWNTOWN
Westfield
E. Broad St.

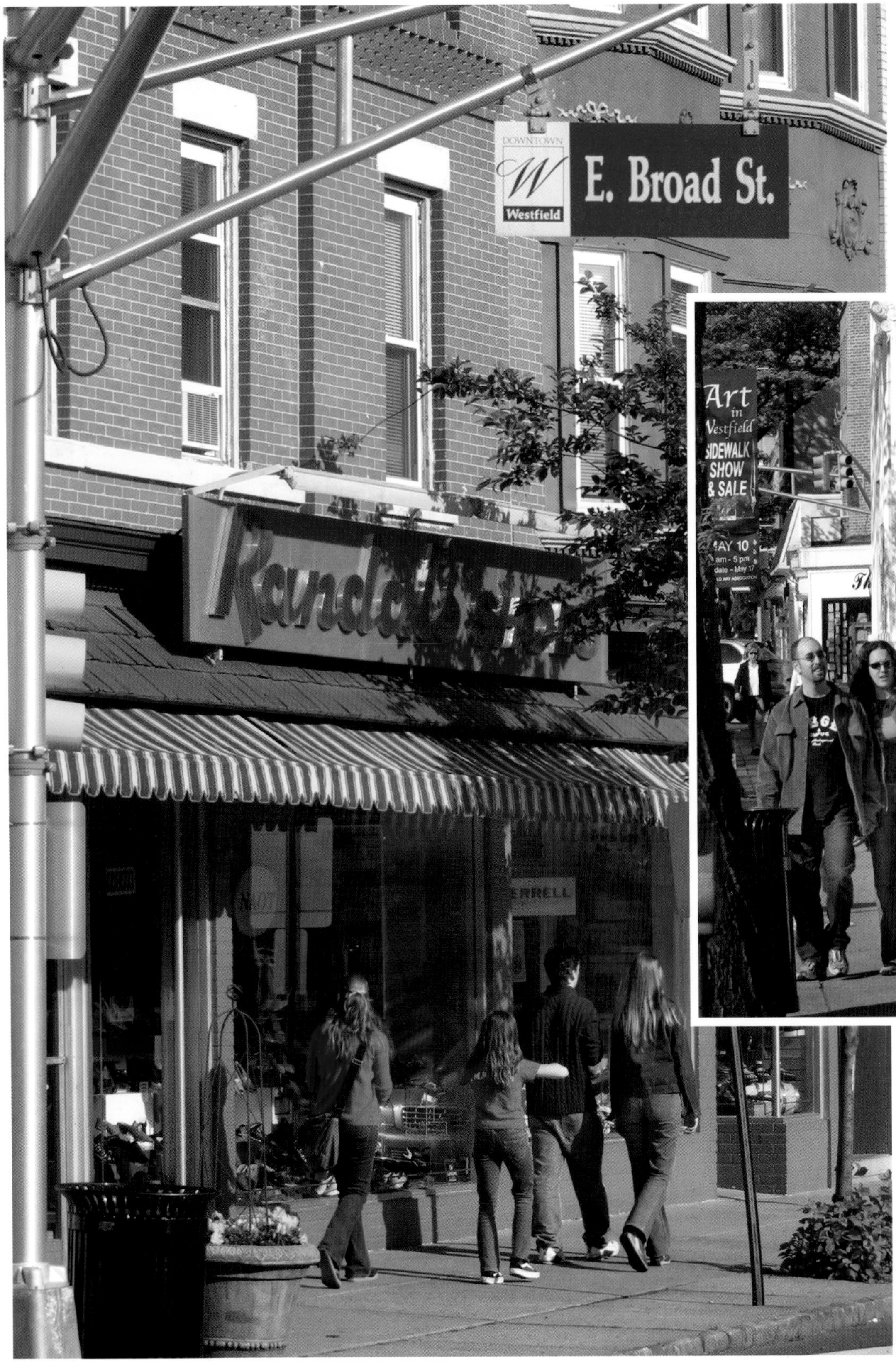

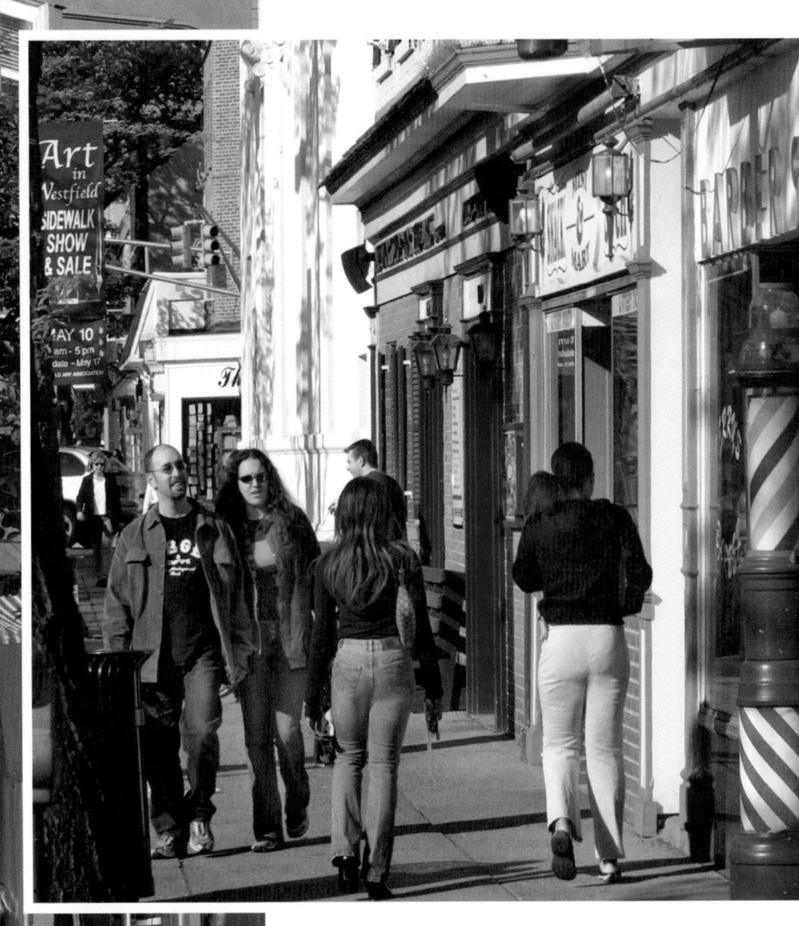

Art in Westfield
SIDEWALK SHOW & SALE

Downtown
Westfield

Westfield "Y"

ONLY
ONLY

Aerial of Westfield

Soccer,
Houlihan Field

Soccer,
Tamaques Park

Soccer, Elm Street Field

Yard sales

Notable Homes Tour,
Friends of
Westfield Symphony

Tamaques Park

Crossing at
Broad & Central

Miller-Cory House Museum

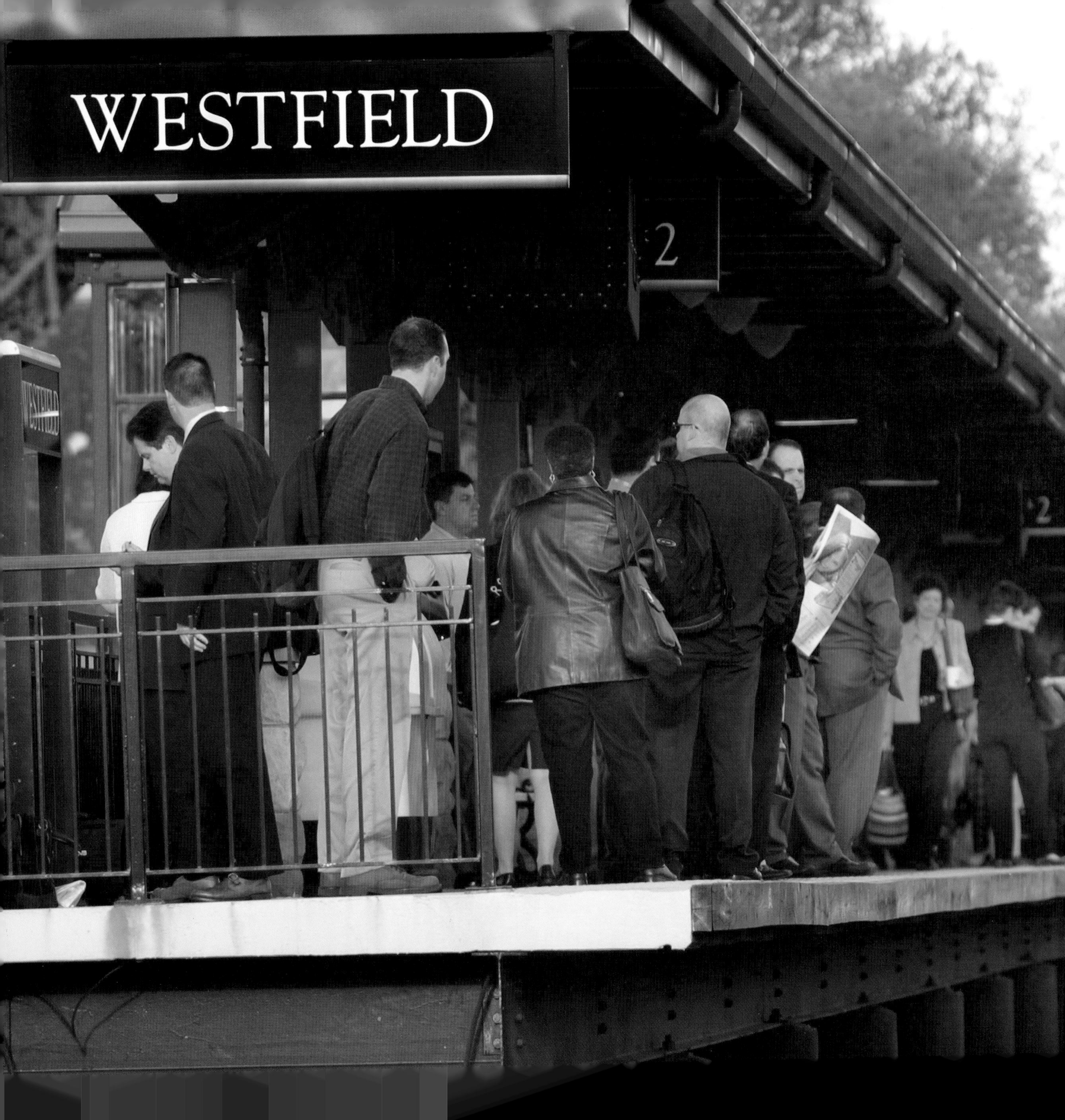
WESTFIELD
2
WESTFIELD
2

Westfield
Train Station

Spring,
Mindowaskin Park

Chief John Castellano, and members of Westfield Fire Department

Westfield Fire Department

Bovella's Pastry Shoppe

Brummer's Chocolates

Prospect Street

James Ward Mansion, East Broad Street

Brightwood Park

NO
ROLLERBLADING
OR
SKATEBOARDING
PERMITTED

Westfield High School

Memorial Day wreaths, The Plaza

September 11th Memorial Park

Canada Geese,
Mindowaskin
Park

Lacrosse,
Edison School
& Keehler Field

Westfield
High School
Graduation

Project Graduation "BASH",
Optimist Club

EHIGH
PDA

Nancy Priest and Sherry Cronin

Mindowaskin Park Overlook,
Friends of Mindowaskin Park

Grace Orthodox
Presbyterian Church

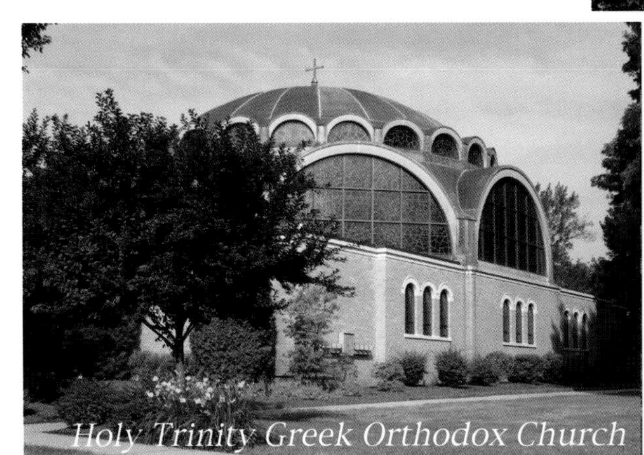
Holy Trinity Greek Orthodox Church

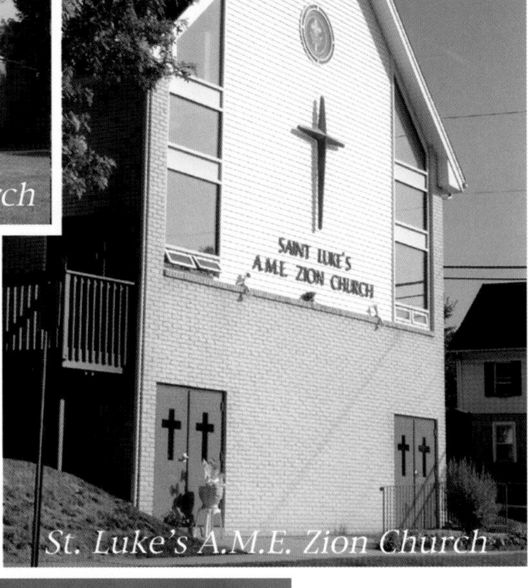

St. Luke's A.M.E. Zion Church

Christadelphian Chapel

Bethel Baptist Church

First United Methodist Church

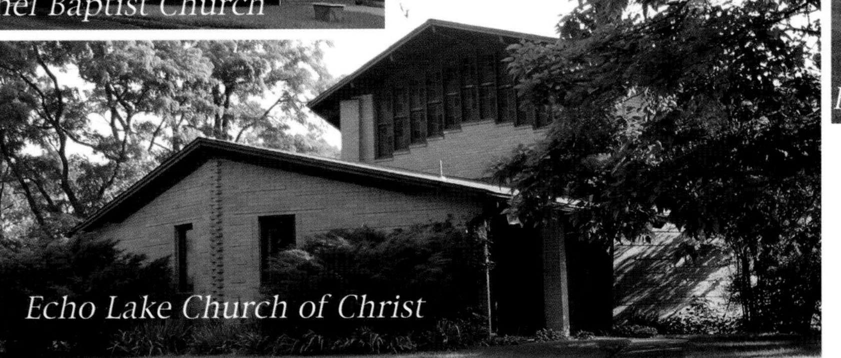
Echo Lake Church of Christ

First Congregational Church

Westfield
houses of worship

The Presbyterian Church of Westfield

Westfield Post Office

Westfield Fire Department

Manor Park Swim Club

Flags box at Fire Department

Baseball,
Tamaques Park

Softball,
Tamaques Park

Greek Festival,
Holy Trinity Greek
Orthodox Church

The
LEADER STORE
University Shop
BOYS & MENS
WEAR
ENTRANCE AROUND THE CORNER
EXIT
LANES
THOU SHAL
NOT
PARK
HERE
KIMBALL CIRCLE
WESTFIELD TOWN BELL
CAST IN 1869 BY VICKERS FOUNDRY, SHEFFIELD, ENGLAND
1869 - 1921 HUNG IN PROSPECT ST. SCHOOL. SERVED AS SCHOOL BELL, TOWN BELL, FIRE BELL.
1922 - 1985 HUNG IN MADISON AVE. PRESBYTERIAN CHAPEL
1994 RESTORED FOR WESTFIELD BICENTENNIAL BY WESTFIELD HISTORICAL SOCIETY & TOWN D.P.W.
JOHN R. PANOSH - TOWN BELLMASTER
RALPH H. JONES - TOWN HISTORIAN RICHARD EDGE - D.P.W.
WESTFIELD
RESCUE SQUAD
VOLUNTEER
EMERGENCY MEDICAL SERVICE
WESTFIELD SERVICE LEAGUE
THRIFT SHOP
AND
CONSIGNMENT
SHOP
RIALTO
BOULEVARD
BENEATH THIS BOULDER
A TIME CAPSULE WAS PLACED IN
NOVEMBER 1983
TO CLOSE
WESTFIELD'S BICENTENNIAL OBSERVANCE
IT IS TO BE OPENED
WESTFIELD HISTORICAL SOCIETY
SITES OF
OLD TOWN TAVERN
1760
STAGE COACH DAYS
WESTFIELD INN
MATTHIAS CLARK
MEMORIAL PARK
BEST WESTERN
WESTFIELD
INN
MANOR PARK
SWIM CLUB
W
WESTFIELD
1720
YEH, BUT TRADER JOE'S IS DEFINITELY WORTH IT...
WE'VE BEEN WALKING FOR DAYS.
506
NOMAHEGAN
SWIM CLUB
MEMBERS ONLY
WESTFIELD
MEMORIAL
POOL

Linda Maggio

Autumn,
Mindowaskin Park

Cooking class, Classic Thyme

Frazee Barn, Miller-Cory House Museum

Presbyterian Church
Revolutionary Cemetery

Fairview Cemetery

School tours, Westfield Historical Society

Reeve Home, Westfield Historical Society

Ralph H. Jones,
Town Historian,
Archives of Westfield
Historical Society

Historic Westfield

In 1664 English settlers from Long Island purchased the Elizabethtown tract from the Lenape chieftains. Over the next half century the west fields of Elizabethtown were surveyed and divided until early pioneers cleared enough land for Westfield to become a distinct settlement in 1720.

During the American Revolution, Westfield was a command post and the village was occupied and looted by the main British Army in June of 1777. In 1780 Westfielders participated in the victorious Battle of Springfield.

Westfield was a small farming village and stagecoach stop through the late 18th and early 19th centuries but flourished from the introduction of the Elizabethtown and Somerville Railroad in 1838, which later became the Central Railroad of New Jersey. As railroad networks expanded into the early 20th century, Westfield grew as well, experiencing its golden age of prosperity.

The Westfield Historical Society maintains the largest archives of Westfield lore, including artifacts, memorabilia, documents and photographs. Thanks to the generosity and cooperation of the Westfield Historical Society, the following historical photographs present a contrasting view of Westfield's past.

Photo: Lower Westfield Avenue

Gideon Ross Esq., Ross Manor, *circa* 1860s

Wittke Garden, *circa* 1910

Robert M. French Home, Central Avenue, *circa* 1890s

Westfield High School, 1917

Miss Moore's School, *circa* 1900

Lincoln School (original), Temple Place, 1890s

Prospect Street School, *circa* 1898

Lincoln School, 2nd grade knitters, 1941

Lincoln School, *circa* 1905

Lusardi Confectionary & E. L. Sanders Cigar Store, Welcome Home Celebration, October 1919

Broad & Elm Streets, October 1919

Circus, Broad Street looking west, 1918

Westfield Club, 1897

Elm Lawn Tennis Club, First Tournament, July 4, 1885

First Westfield Symphony, 1923

Girl's Track Team, 1924

Rotary Club Regatta, 1923

Elmer Chattin, WHS Captain, 1922

Independent Order of Stars, Ice Hockey Team, December 25, 1897

Boys Athletic Club Football Team, 1910

J. Dickson Westfield Dairy delivery wagons, Broad Street, *circa* 1910

Snyder City Market,
206 E. North Avenue,
circa 1910

Scudder's Cash Market, 9 Elm Street, *circa* 1915

North Avenue
Fire House,
circa 1900

Bellini Westfield Italian Band, Professor Gaetano Mannino, *circa* 1920

Westfield Police Department, 1914

Burhans Residence, 417 Prospect Street, 1914

Senator James Miller residence, Elm Street, 1880s

Corner of Hazel Avenue and 1st Street, 1912

DOWNTOWN WESTFIELD CORPORATION
Photo Contest Winners

"9-11 Memorial"
Joey & Ali Quintero
Grand Prize Winner

"The Parade"
Anthony Riccio
2nd Place, Events

"Downtown Halloween"
Buoscio
3rd Place, Events

"Westfield Community Band Concert"
Gerry Cleaves
1st Place, Events

"Westfield Fire Station"
David Verchick *(Age 9)*
2nd Place, Details

"TV Show *Ed*"
Cheri Rogowsky
3rd Place, Details

"Turtle at Tamaques Lake"
Evan Falk *(Age 16)*
1st Place, Details

"Fall in Mindowaskin Park"
Chris Forno
2nd Place, Seasons

"Fairview Blossoms"
Millicent Brody
3rd Place, Seasons

"Blizzard of 2003"
Karen Clarkson
1st Place, Seasons

Education Fund of Westfield, Inc.

The Education Fund of Westfield, Inc. was formed in 1991 as a non-profit, philanthropic, community-based organization with a tax-exempt status. Its volunteer member Board of Trustees is independent of the Westfield Board of Education, but works cooperatively with the Board and Administration.

The Education Fund is Westfield's response to the national challenge to keep our young people well equipped and productive in an increasingly competitive, complex and changing world. Its purpose is to provide a catalyst for the generation and allocation of resources to enhance the programs for students of the Westfield Public Schools. It seeks to be a partner of the schools and the community in the pursuit of excellence. The non-profit organization provides an ongoing, centralized source of additional funds and resources to assist the public schools in maintaining and enhancing the quality of education in Westfield.

Supporting Sponsors

Coldwell Banker

Westfield is a wonderful community! Coldwell Banker, the community's premier real estate company, is pleased to support this ambitious project.

Burgdorff ERA Realtors

The Westfield Office salutes this celebration of our hometown and is proud to be a sponsor of this wonderful endeavor.

Optimist Club of Westfield

Westfield Service League

Classic Thyme

The Town Book Store

Westfield Historical Society

Century 21 Taylor & Love

Downtown Westfield Corporation

Friends of Mindowaskin Park

Garden Club of Westfield

Junior League of Elizabeth-Plainfield

Rake and Hoe Garden Club

United Way of Westfield

Westfield Foundation

Westfield Symphony Orchestra

Westfield "Y"

Jayne Bernstein - Coldwell Banker
Hye-Young Choi - Coldwell Banker
Frank D. Isoldi - Coldwell Banker
Mary McEnerney - Coldwell Banker
Eileen Passananti - Coldwell Banker
Michael Scott - Coldwell Banker
Carol Tener - Burgdorff ERA

Peter & Joanne Santoriello
Michael & Darielle Walsh

The Plaza